Original title:
The Ocean's Song of Silence

Copyright © 2025 Creative Arts Management OÜ
All rights reserved.

Author: Alec Davenport
ISBN HARDBACK: 978-1-80587-313-6
ISBN PAPERBACK: 978-1-80587-783-7

Floating on the Breath of Stillness

In the quiet waves, I sway and spin,
A fish with a joke, can't help but grin.
The seaweed dances, trying to groove,
While crabs in tuxedos make quite a move.

A dolphin giggles, flips with glee,
Says, 'Why did the barnacle cross the sea?
To get to the shell, oh what a fate,
But now he's stuck – it's far too late!'

The sun peeks in, with a wink and a smile,
As turtles in shades cruise the surf for a while.
They chuckle and chat as they take a stroll,
While jellyfish float, feeling quite whole.

A seagull squawks, trying too hard,
To impress a shrimp, who's quite a bard.
With a flick of a tail and a splash of charm,
They laugh in the air, sharing their calm.

The Calm Before the Wave's Whisper

A seagull's squawk breaks the hush,
Bubbles float, then begin to rush.
The tide is lazy, not a care,
Yet people jog, they think it's fair.

Fish play poker beneath the tide,
Invisible fins take guests inside.
Crabs in tuxedos dance with flair,
As jellyfish float without a pair.

Twilight's Soft Embrace over the Waters

The sun winks, the sky turns shy,
A clam hums, asking passersby.
Starfish gossip, they're quite the chat,
While dolphins giggle at a fallen hat.

The moon sneezes, sending waves a-skip,
As starry nights invite a dip.
Beneath, the fish throw a grand ball,
And seaweed dances, never to fall.

A Gentle Breath Among the Waves

A lazy breeze whispers sweet jokes,
With turtlenecks worn by funny folks.
Crabs wear hats and dance on the sand,
While barnacles grin, content and grand.

Flip-flops squeak with every stride,
As laughter tumbles in the tide.
Seashells chuckle, their echoes sing,
While sea cucumbers do their thing.

Mysteries Held in Liquid Stillness

Bubbles rise, the secrets swell,
An octopus winks, 'I know it well.'
Seashells giggle like they're in a dream,
While fish form a conga line, a shiny team.

Unseen whispers in the night,
Seaweed sways with pure delight.
The surface calm, but laughs below,
For treasure hunts just steal the show.

Silence Underneath the Beacon's Glow

Beneath the light where sailors dream,
The fish all gossip, or so it seems.
Octopus twirls, a dance so fine,
While crabs critique the fish's design.

Waves gently chuckle, tickling the shore,
As snails write poetry, never a bore.
Clams keep secrets; they're good at that,
While dolphins giggle, wearing a hat.

Distant Dreams on the Open Sea

Whales hum softly, sipping their tea,
While we drift lazily, just you and me.
The gulls are plotting a daring heist,
Stealing our chips; oh, they're quite nice!

Stars blink above, winking in jest,
As jellyfish glow, they're feeling blessed.
Turtles trade jokes in the moon's soft light,
Tides laughing gently at our delight.

The Stillness of Seagulls Roosting

Seagulls are perched, looking so wise,
With beaks like comedians, they tell no lies.
While they pretend to be all serious,
Their squawks remind us it's all delirious.

Feathers a-fluff, they strike a pose,
Trying to impress with their snappy clothes.
One tries to fly, but trips on a wave,
Plunging right down; the crowd must be brave!

Echoes of Respite in the Tempest

Amidst the storm, a clam does snore,
While otters play cards on a tossing floor.
Waves grumble grumpily, but who can tell?
The sea's just joking, under its spell.

Squid share tall tales with each other near,
While a sea cucumber rolls with cheer.
Barnacles mutter about the weather,
Grumpy old shells, stuck there together.

Beneath the Calm, a Gentle Whim

Bubbles rise with each soft sway,
A fishy dance on a lazy day.
Seagulls squawk, but seem confused,
They battle waves, but feel bemused.

Crabs in hats, all strut and prance,
They've got the moves, they'll take a chance.
A quicksand tango, oh what a sight,
With beach ball dreams, they own the night.

Traces of Tranquility on the Dunes

Footprints lead to a sandwich grave,
Forgotten lunch, oh how they wave!
A crab waves back, in jest and cheer,
"That ham and cheese is way too dear!"

Sandy castles with moat in tow,
Mermaids laugh, then steal the show.
A seagull yawns, then takes a dive,
Dish-sharing dreams, they stay alive.

The Wayward Wings of Silent Currents

A jellyfish floats, all soft and sly,
Winking like it's the star of the sky.
I'd join its dance, but my legs are stuck,
In a tangle of seaweed - oh, what bad luck!

The starfish grins, it knows the trick,
It plays the harmonica, quick and slick.
With a wink and a wiggle, it steals the show,
Beneath the waves, they all dare to glow.

Melancholy Under the Midnight Sea

Nautilus dreamed of a briny spree,
While octopuses planned their next tea.
Clams played cards, but lost their shells,
Sneaky little fish rang dinner bells.

The tides whisper jokes in a salty hum,
As a grumpy tortoise just won't come.
With the stars above, it seems so surreal,
But that crustacean's snore is quite the deal!

Lullaby of the Endless Horizons

Waves giggle as they reach the shore,
Whispers of secrets from the ocean floor.
Seagulls dance like it's a show,
While fish play tag beneath the glow.

Sandy toes and laughter loud,
Seashells echo, feeling proud.
The tide brings in a salty breeze,
Tickling noses, oh what a tease!

Melodies of the Submerged World

Bubble-blowers in an underwater spree,
Dancing seaweed sways just for me.
Crabs wear hats that make us grin,
With tiny jokes that always win.

Octopuses play peek-a-boo,
While clams sing songs, just a few.
Fish are bopping to the beat,
Underwater parties can't be beat!

Softness Cradled by Tides

The tide pulls gently at my feet,
Shells whisper secrets, oh so sweet.
Starfish giggle, making a scene,
With little dances, they're quite keen.

As I drift in, seahorses wave,
In this world, there's joy to save.
Floating dreams in the briny blue,
Where laughter lives, and skies are true.

Silence Amongst Coral Castles

Coral towers rise to the sky,
Fish parade, waving their goodbye.
Anemones tickle with a smile,
While dolphins jump in playful style.

Crabs throw parties, oh what a bash,
With hermit friends, they make a splash.
In stillness found beneath the waves,
Funny creatures, their antics saves!

Whispering Blue of Forgotten Shores

Once a fish wore a tiny hat,
It swam with style, imagine that!
Seagulls laughed, they flapped and flew,
While crabs danced in their shellfish shoes.

Turtles tell tales of deep sea pranks,
Of octopuses in bubble tanks.
The sand giggles, tickles the toes,
As waves whisper secrets, nobody knows.

Embrace of the Tidal Breeze

A jellyfish floats, a true ballet,
Inviting all to join the play.
But watch your toes, they sting quite well,
While dolphins ring a silly bell.

With starfish lounging on sunlit rocks,
Counting crabs as they take their walks.
The breeze pulls pranks on weary sails,
As laughter echoes in fishy trails.

Unheard Conversations in Vast Waters

The deep is filled with quirks untold,
A clam recites, but it's quite bold.
A snail sings softly, just out of tune,
While barnacles hum beneath the moon.

Whales bring whispers from the dark,
Of mermaids misplacing their spark.
The waves just roll their watery eyes,
As fish giggle at the passing skies.

The Quiet Dance of Nautical Shadows

A shadowy squid in a top hat spins,
While seahorses learn to do the kin.
Lobsters giggle, wearing their shells,
As mackerel tell the tallest tales.

The seaweed sways, like a groovy dude,
In a dance-off that looks rather rude.
With every splash and flicking tail,
The ocean chuckles, it can't curtail.

Under the Currents

Waves whisper secrets, oh so sly,
Fish wear sunglasses, as they swim by.
Crabs dance to tunes only they know,
Making a scene in the water's glow.

Seagulls crack jokes, landing with flair,
While starfish play poker, with a wild stare.
A turtle in shades takes a midday nap,
Dreaming of tacos, or a fishy wrap.

A Gentle Peace

Bubbles giggle, drifting away,
A clam throws a party, come what may.
The sand tickles toes, in a sly jest,
While jellyfish bounce, feeling quite blessed.

Shells gossip loudly, sharing a laugh,
As dolphins perform their splashy craft.
Under this light, nothing feels wrong,
Every wave cradles a cheerful song.

Chasing Shadows on Silent Waters

A shadow dances, could be a seal,
Or just a waterlogged, squishy meal.
Gaze at the waves, where shadows fly,
Maybe it's just a catfish gone high!

With every ripple, a new tale unfolds,
Of pirate ducks and mermaids bold.
They squawk and they bubble, a quirky delight,
Under the sun, everything feels right.

A Symphony of Softly Falling Waves

The waves tap-dance, one-two-three,
While crabs conduct, sipping iced tea.
Fish form a band, scales shimmering bright,
Each plop and splish feels just right.

A seaweed saxophonist plays a tune,
While clams improvise under the moon.
It's all a show that brings such glee,
Even the oysters join in with a spree!

Under the Moon's Quiet Gaze

Moonbeams tickle, as they softly play,
While fish have a picnic, enjoying their stay.
The turtles are gossiping, bright shells aglow,
All are invited to the sandcastle show.

Starfish are kings, on a throned rock chair,
Regaling their subjects, a grand tale to share.
What happens in water, stays here, it's true,
Especially when sea cucumbers brew!

Celestial Silence Above the Waves

In the sky, fish whisper jokes,
While the crabs giggle in their cloaks.
Seagulls squawk like a choir gone mad,
As dolphins dance, though it's kinda bad.

The clouds take naps, drifting like dreams,
While octopuses plot with their schemes.
Starfish hold secrets, trying to be sly,
While the tide just rolls on by, oh my!

Echoes of Solitude and Serenity

Turtles tell tales of old sea lore,
And fish wear glasses, what a bore!
A clam tried singing its favorite tune,
But the seaweed scoffed, 'That's not a boon!'

Drifting by jellyfish in their gowns,
With jellybeans floating, oh, what clowns!
The snails race slow, they're late for their date,
While sea cucumbers just contemplate.

Tranquil Depths of the Water's Heart

Bubbles pop like laughter in the deep,
As starry-eyed fish just barely peep.
The waves play tag, splashing with glee,
While sea horses argue, 'Who's faster, me?'

Crabs crack jokes with a pinch of salt,
While plankton swirl in a waltz, oh what a fault!
The sharks sit back, in their shades so grand,
Sipping on seawater from a laid-back stand.

Mysteries in the Ocean's Veil

Mermaids throw parties with guppy delight,
While blowfish puff up, trying to fright.
Walruses wear hats atop their heads,
While the sea foam giggles and spins in beds.

Dolphins play tricks, making waves with sheer joy,
As starfish debate who's a good decoy.
The anchor's lost - or was it the boat?
But who needs rules on this funny float?

Canvases of Still Waters

In the quiet where fish like to sway,
A duck sings off-key, brightening the gray.
The turtles wear glasses, so wise and so old,
While the catfish tell tales that are never quite bold.

The sun sneezes softly, the waves say, 'Bless you!'
Jellyfish giggles and squishy fish stew.
With umbrellas of seaweed, the crabs have their fun,
As they dance in the sun, oh, what a pun!

Waterscapes of Serenity and Solitude

Stars in the water, they swim in reverse,
While the seaweed's a poet, writing verses diverse.
The mermaids are napping, adorned in seagrass,
Snoring in bubbles, they dream 'bout the past.

The dolphins are surfers, on waves made of foam,
Crashing for laughs in their underwater home.
The starfish are judges for the best clams' dance,
But the sea cucumbers refuse to take a chance!

The Whisper of a Forgotten Shore

On the sand where sea roaches play peek-a-boo,
The crabs recite poetry, a funny haiku.
Seashells gossip loudly under the moon's glow,
As the waves try to shovel the sand for a show.

Old flip-flops converse, in pairs they debate,
Which way to head home, or tempting to wait?
Seagulls steal fries from sunbathers below,
While the tide sings a tune with a comical flow!

Nocturnal Echoes Amidst the Tides

At night, the waves giggle, they tickle the land,
While the crickets join in with their musical band.
The moon plays a gig on its silvery shell,
And the eels pull the strings, oh, what a swell!

The stars twinkle brightly, like winks from a friend,
As the shadows dance lightly, their moves never end.
In laughter and whispers, the sea holds us tight,
It's a quirky parade through the warm summer night!

Murmurs of Seagrass Dreams

Underwater grass sways and bends,
Fish gossip softly, make amends.
Seahorses dance, in silly delight,
Waves of laughter, a funny sight.

A crab plays peek-a-boo with a shell,
While jellyfish float, they giggle as well.
Starfish plotting a tickle attack,
In this quiet world, there's no turning back.

Anemones tickle with touch so light,
Clams hold in chuckles, try with all might.
The seaweed whispers, secrets to keep,
While dolphins giggle in a bubble of sleep.

The Quiet Heart of the Abyss

In the deep, where whispers sway,
A fish tells tales, in a sly way.
Octopus riddles and wraps up tight,
Turns into chaos, such a strange sight.

Giant squids make a mess with ink,
Bubble-makers float, let their thoughts sink.
A turtle snickers behind a stone,
As crabs form a band, all on their own.

Mollusks gossip, secrets to share,
A barnacle laughs, without a care.
In the quiet dark, with echoes they play,
Tickles and giggles lead the way.

Reflection in Celestial Ripples

Bubbles rise, like balloons of cheer,
Reflecting laughter, oh so dear.
A school of fish with synchronized moves,
Dancing in patterns, making their grooves.

A sea turtle wears a goofy grin,
As the tide rolls in, let the fun begin.
The coral reefs hum a lively tune,
Under the light of a shimmering moon.

A playful dolphin, flips in delight,
Telling jokes in the soft starlight.
Gifts of silliness float on a breeze,
Tickling waves, putting hearts at ease.

Harmonies in the Briny Depths

Down below where the silliness hums,
A clownfish juggles, and everyone drums.
Sea urchins giggle, dressed up so fine,
In the depths, every creature can shine.

Puffers inflate, just for a tease,
While stingrays glide with incredible ease.
The sand dollar spins, just for a laugh,
All gather 'round for a sea critters' bath.

Leaping through waves, like children at play,
With harmonies sweet, they start their ballet.
A symphony found in the quiet abyss,
Making music that none could dismiss.

Songs of Stillness in the Blue Expanse

Bubbles dance, they laugh and tease,
With seaweed wigs and jellyfish ease.
Crabs in tuxedos, quite a sight,
Having a gala in soft moonlight.

Turtles wearing shades, oh so cool,
Sipping seawater, breaking the rule.
Fish gossiping in coral bars,
Counting grains of sand like distant stars.

Starfish tossing a beach-ball high,
Playing catch with the seagull fly.
Whales are whispering silly things,
Sharing secrets and fishy flings.

Anemones wave like glamour stars,
While clowns parade in their little cars.
In this blue world where turtles run,
The joke's on us, it's all just fun!

The Hushed Breath of Nautical Realms

Dolphins giggle, flip through the spray,
Planting pranks in their splashy way.
Octopuses juggling with such flair,
Throwing ink blots, without a care.

Seahorses waltz in a tangled ballet,
Making mermaids roll their eyes and sway.
Crabs lounge around, gossiping slow,
While starfish miss the summer show.

From the depths, a clam's loud snore,
Echoes softly, ask for more.
So quiet down here, it's quite absurd,
As silence dances, not a word heard.

Waves chuckle softly, a gentle tease,
While sand dollars plot to spread the breeze.
This watery realm, a chuckling place,
Where silence wears a funny face.

Languid Whispers from the Underworld

In murky depths where shadows creep,
A fishy joke causes a raucous peep.
Ghostly squids paint the dark with glee,
As bubbles giggle, 'Can you see me?'

Eels tangled up in a riddle game,
Slither and grin, no two the same.
Mollusks sing tunes so offbeat,
Even sea stars dance to the off-beat.

A lazy whale hums his favorite tune,
Seducing fish into a comical swoon.
An urchin claims he's a movie star,
But really, he's just a spiky car.

This underworld replete with jest,
Where silence takes a humorous rest.
As currents weave tales both tricky and sly,
In the stillness, laughter seems to swim by.

Timeless Silence in Aquatic Dreams

A sea cucumber pondered, quite confused,
Why all the fish were so well amused.
With quiet hope, he tip-toed near,
Only to find that laughter's here!

Whales whisper puns to the rolling tide,
While dolphins giggle and dance with pride.
Crabs on the shore putting on a show,
With punchlines crafted from shells they know.

Even the barnacles join in too,
Telling tales of what only they knew.
Hermit crabs swap shells with a flair,
And giggle when seagulls throw temper flair.

In this world of silence, laughter swells,
A melody formed from the ocean's bells.
So in the depths, where stillness gleams,
It's really just life, in aquatic dreams.

Shimmering Shadows of Tranquility

Bubbles dance and giggle loud,
Fish wear hats, they feel so proud.
Starfish play a secret game,
While crabs insist it's all the same.

Seagulls drop their snacks with flair,
Octopuses plotting in mid-air.
The tides make waves, a proper fuss,
While turtles yawn, all nonchalant, thus.

The Still Voice of Distant Shores

Waves whisper jokes to sandy toes,
A conch shell sings, 'Just strike a pose!'
Clams gossip over shells, quite neat,
While dolphins dance to a jazzy beat.

Seashells hum with a cheeky grin,
As barnacles groan, 'Where to begin?'
The wind spills secrets, quite absurd,
A crab chuckles, 'Have you heard?'

Secrets Carried by Gentle Currents

Seaweed sways in a dapper suit,
Fish practice their ballerina loot.
The tide winks flirtatiously at the moon,
While hermit crabs party - a sandy tune!

Jellyfish jiggle, oh what a sight,
They throw a rave, glowing so bright.
The water swirls with giggles and glee,
Waves roll their eyes, 'Oh, let it be!'

Unspoken Truths of the Sea's Embrace

Whales chuckle with tales of the deep,
While fishes argue about who to keep.
The tide loves to tease and pull,
It snaps back, 'Don't be such a fool!'

Coral reefs gossip, all in good fun,
As plankton twirls, soaking up sun.
The ocean chuckles, a bubbling brews,
With every wave, it shares its muse.

Secrets of the Deep

Bubbles rise, fish hold their breath,
A shark sneezes, oh what a mess!
Starfish giggle, clinging to rock,
Jellyfish waltz, tickling the flock.

Seahorses dance with great delight,
Clams just snore, sleeping through night.
An octopus paints with its ink,
While crabs just stop and laugh, I think!

Whales hum tunes from ancient times,
Dolphins chuckle in joyful climbs.
But watch out for the seashell's glare,
It tells tales of mermaids' crazy hair!

The deep sea's secrets are never boring,
With every splash, there's someone soaring.
As fish share jokes we can't quite hear,
In the vast expanse, there's always cheer!

Melodies of the Still Waters

Ripples dance where ducks play peek,
Frogs croak tunes, though out of beat.
A fish dives deep for a tasty snack,
While turtles lounge, relaxing on back.

The quiet hum of calm delights,
Sailor's cap forgotten in sights.
And every wave a giggle makes,
As friendly otters share their cakes.

The moonlight sings on silvery waves,
While lazy catsnap sailors' braves.
With crickets tapping their secret song,
It's funny how nature hums along!

So lift your voice, don't hold it in,
In still waters, let laughter begin.
For every wave has a story told,
Of moments shared, both funny and bold!

Solitude of the Sea

A lone fish wonders 'where's my crew?'
Seagulls cackle at a seaweed stew.
A ship's wheel spins, no one in sight,
As waves applaud for the lonely plight.

Barnacles gossip, stuck on the hull,
While crabs play cards, and nobody's dull.
The sun drops low, it's time to dine,
As sailors dream of the fish that shine.

In solitude, the sea finds mirth,
Anemones sway, full of worth.
And even the tide knows how to jest,
Bringing laughter, a welcome guest.

So embrace the quiet, the space between,
For solitude's charm is rarely seen.
With each wave's whisper, there's joy and flair,
In the vastness, fun is always there!

Calm Between the Currents

Between the currents, life drifts slow,
A starfish waves, says 'hello!'
Seaweed dances like it's on air,
While snails plot schemes with utmost care.

Fish compete for the funniest face,
An eel slides in with a sneaky grace.
And while the tide takes a little nap,
The sea turtles share a funny clap.

The bubbles form a comedic mask,
It's tough to find a quiet task.
As whispers float on a gentle breeze,
All creatures find humor with such ease.

So when you wander by the blue,
Remember the laughter in every hue.
The calm between holds jokes galore,
In the watery world, there's always more!

Quietude of the Forgotten Shore

Upon the sand, the seagulls cheer,
A beach ball rolls—it disappears!
The crabs perform their sideways dance,
While sunburnt folks just take a chance.

A flip-flop flies, an awkward swoop,
The kids all laugh, quite like a troupe.
A starfish looks, bemused and shy,
Wondering why we scream and cry.

The tide it tickles, waves do creep,
As sandcastles start to weep.
In this calm, we find our fate,
What's left behind? A fishy plate!

But here we sit, in blissful craze,
The ocean's joke, a salty haze.
We laugh at waves that quirk and plunge,
Oh, quietude, let's all get grunge!

Harmonic Drift of Water's Muse

Bubbles bubble, fishy tunes,
A whale's face looks like a balloon!
Mermaids giggle, splashing wide,
While sailors swear, their boats can't glide.

A lighthouse winks, a cheeky beam,
As dolphins join in on the theme.
With octopuses, hats askew,
They play charades in ocean blue.

The kraken's laugh—so deep it goes,
While barnacles gossip, who knows?
Each splash a note, each tide a rhyme,
In this watery world, we waste our time.

But oh, the joy of nautical jest,
In silent waves, we find our rest.
With each crab dance and stormy air,
We share the humor hidden there!

The Invisible Choir of Ocean Depths

Down below where shadows play,
An echo sings, come what may.
Squid squirt ink in a concert hall,
While clownfish giggle at it all.

The eels electrify the night,
Creating tunes that feel just right.
A pufferfish fills up with glee,
For curvy lines in a fishy spree.

Invisible voices serenade,
In bubbling whispers, dreams are made.
The coral's gossip, a vibrant shush,
While jellyfish float without a rush.

So close your eyes, let laughter swell,
Amongst the sea, all's well, so well.
For silence in waves spins tales untold,
With giggles lurking, brave and bold!

Serenity Beneath the Surface

Beneath the waves, a dance unfolds,
With sea turtles telling tales of old.
Starfish lounging, sun-kissed and bright,
A clam just claps; it's quite the sight!

Bubbles float like giggles near,
As fishes whisper what they hear.
One fish shouts, "Why's the water cold?"
Another answers, "It's magic, I'm told!"

Dolphins leap, a splashy trace,
Turning the sea into a race.
While sea anemones tease and sway,
As if to say, "Come dance and play!"

So here we drift with silly grins,
In the quiet where laughter begins.
Wave after wave, we find our peace,
Wonders of silence never cease!

Whispers Beneath the Waves

Fish gossip in bubbles, oh what a sight,
Crabs snap at secrets, in the moonlight.
Starfish throw shade, that's one great pun,
While shrimps do the cha-cha, isn't this fun?

Turtles talk slow, like they're on a stroll,
Jellyfish glide by with a squishy role.
Seahorses giggle, what a peculiar team,
Clams keep it hush, they've lost their dream.

In the back, a whale cracks a joke so loud,
While seaweed dances, feeling quite proud.
They chuckle 'til dawn, it's a watery show,
And the tide rolls in with a comedic flow.

So listen up close, hear the waves softly chime,
Every splash and ripple is simply sublime.
In this bubbly expanse, laughter takes flight,
Where silence is funny, and the sea feels just right.

Rhythm of the Deep Blue Calm

Underwater knock-knock jokes bubble and rise,
The octopus winks with eight clever eyes.
Dolphins are dancing, flipping with glee,
While seagulls crack jokes about salty brie.

Whales harmonize in a goofy choir,
Splashing around like they're on fire.
Manta rays glide with an elegant twist,
While bubbles in sync play a comic list.

Eels wear their best ties, looking so fine,
While anemones giggle, drinking sea brine.
A lobster sips tea, feeling quite sappy,
As the tides chuckle quietly, all feeling happy.

In this calm rhythm, laughter sways near,
With crabs pinching jokes for all to hear.
The deep blue water holds secrets so tight,
Yet somehow it makes every moment feel bright.

Echoes in Still Waters

The goldfish chatter in their little bowls,
Trading silly stories with goofy roles.
Puffers puff up when they get a joke,
And minnows break dance, it's quite the folk.

The quietest pond, where the frogs like to croak,
Hosts wild debates over which fly is a joke.
Lily pads nod, as if to agree,
That life beneath ripples is a grand comedy.

In the stillness arrives a turtle so wise,
With punchlines that catch every listener by surprise.
While the water reflects every chuckle and wink,
Making ripples of laughter, more profound than we think.

So lean by the banks, let the giggles cascade,
In echoes of humor, no need to masquerade.
For silence is crafty, with whispers, we play,
And the depths of the water hold laughter at bay.

Serenade of the Moonlit Sea

Under the moonlight, sardines pirouette,
While sneaky little shrimp play a game of tag, yet.
A dolphin hums softly, a tuning fork song,
With the starfish all clapping, they can't go wrong.

In tidal ballets, crabs twirl in delight,
As waves throw confetti on this magical night.
Sea urchins gossip in their spiky attire,
While rock pools echo with laughter and fire.

An octopus juggles with a flair so grand,
While the sunken treasure holds a comical band.
It's a nautical circus, so bright and so clear,
As the moon winks down, lending ear to the cheer.

Underneath waves, humor floats so free,
Where silence dances wildly, don't you agree?
For in this serenade, laughter's the key,
And the night wraps the ocean in joyful esprit.

The Sound of Water's Embrace

Bubbles dance, with giggles galore,
Turtlenecks whirl, on a sandy floor.
Starfish chat over clam's old tales,
While seahorses waltz on swirling trails.

Octopus juggles with a wink and a grin,
As crabs tell stories of home on the tin.
The seaweed sways, a green disco ball,
Even the tides join in on the call.

A crab with a hat, quite the sight to see,
Sips on a cocktail made of sea debris.
Fish wear sunglasses, taking a break,
In this underwater party, make no mistake.

Laughter bubbles up, like waves on the shore,
The ocean's a jester, always wanting more.
In depths of the blue, the fun never ends,
Where everyone's welcome, and silence transcends.

Shadows of Silence Beneath the Foam.

In the depth of the sea, shadows dance sly,
A fish wearing glasses, oh my, oh my!
With sea cucumber jokes, they lighten the gloom,
Spreading their laughter all over the room.

A dolphin dives deep, not missing a beat,
Singing fish jokes that are quite hard to beat.
The sea turtles chuckle, becoming the kings,
Of all things that bubble, the joy that it brings.

Starfish play poker, with shells as their chips,
While whales on the sidelines take sips and dips.
The current flows gently, it wiggles and waves,
As seagrass all sways, laughing out of their caves.

Amidst all the silence, humor takes flight,
Turning the shadows to pure, vibrant light.
In this watery world, where silliness reigns,
The ocean does giggle; it sparkles and gains.

Whispers Beneath the Waves

A crab on a quest for the world's fanciest hat,
Stocks up on shells, quite the oceanic spat.
With two fish as tailors, they stitch and they sew,
Giggling softly, making a grand show.

Eels play charades, they twist and they twine,
While jellyfish twinkle, looking so divine.
A blubbering whale cracks jokes from the dark,
As sea urchins chuckle, adding their spark.

With the sway of the kelp, the jokes ebb and flow,
A clownfish joins in with a colorful glow.
Sharing the laughter that bubbles up free,
As the whispering waves sing a jolly decree.

From coral to kelp, humor runs rife,
In the depths where the ripples bring ocean life.
So listen closely, to the giggles and plays,
In the quiet of blue, find the laughter it sways.

Serenade of the Untouched Depths

Down deep in the dark, where sea critters thrive,
A walrus sings songs that make all feel alive.
With a wink and a flipper, he starts off the show,
The snickers of fish spark the giggles below.

A hermit crab holds a shell-made parade,
While clownfish throw confetti, but they never fade.
Dancing among rocks, they twirl with delight,
In a symphony of shadows, oh what a sight!

The sea floor erupts in a fun-loving cheer,
As creatures of all kinds simply disappear.
Playing hide and seek, in a game made of glee,
The laughter ignites through the salt of the sea.

In the hush of the waves, a toe-tapping tune,
Beneath the blue depths, life carries a boon.
So join in the fun, in the stillness of deep,
Where the serenade swells and the silliness leaps.

Solace in the Riptide's Hold

Waves giggle and toss like kids at play,
Water swirls, it seems to say,
"Oh dear, not again!" it laughs in delight,
As beach balls drift far out of sight.

Crabs dance to a tune, oh what a sight!
Seagulls roll their eyes, perched high in flight,
"You call that a move?" they squawk with glee,
While fish just bubble, sipping their tea.

Tides come and go, a synchrony weird,
Sandcastles crumble, yet still we cheered,
With buckets in hand, we chase down the fun,
As the sun winks and begins to run.

Oh, the tales the sea whispers, can you hear?
Like socks in the wash, it draws us near,
In laughter and splashes, we all unite,
To dance with the waves, from day until night.

Beneath the Still Surface, a Timeless World

A sea cucumber snores with a soft, sleepy sound,
While jellyfish float like they're lost, round and round,
Coral laughs quietly in shades of bright pink,
Where fish in tuxedos sip on a drink.

Clams keep their secrets, tucked in their shells,
While octopuses tell tales, weaving their spells,
"What's a fish's favorite class?" one giggles in reply,
"Swim-phony!" bubbles rise as they all sigh.

Starfish rehearse ballet under the moon,
While seaweed twirls to an unheard tune,
Crabs clap their claws; what a sight to behold,
As bubbles burst forth like stories retold.

Fish argue their colors, their scales on display,
"I bet I can splash better!" they shout in playful fray,
With grins and bright smiles, they wade through the fun,
In this world beneath waves, we can't help but run.

Serenity of the Celestial Blue

In blue depths lies a party, what's that? A whale!
It's juggling the fish, it's quite the tale,
A dolphin leaps high, wearing shades of cool,
While turtles debate who's the fastest in school.

A crab sidesteps into a flounder's space,
"Excuse me, I'm busy!" it shouts, just in case,
The ocean rolls laughter, in waves soft and keen,
As shells tell their stories, and sand glimmers sheen.

Zebras of the sea mingle, colors all bright,
"You think you can dance?" they joke through the night,
As bubbles of laughter escape from the deep,
With currents that swirl, they gather and leap.

With winds that play tunes, the sea takes a bow,
Leaving sea foam applause, a final wow,
Where every wave glimmers like jokes told anew,
In this world of wonders, it's just me and you.

Unspoken Moments at Dusk's Edge

At dusk, the ocean throws the best of her tales,
With glittering stars that dance in the gales,
A clam glances shyly, blushes so red,
While crabs hold their breaths, a spiny parade.

The sun bows low, in a grand, golden flurry,
Gulls laugh over fish, causing quite the hurry,
A turtle in pink says, "What's on the menu?"
Splashing and giggling, with friends, just a few.

A hermit crab struts in a shell far too grand,
"I'm the new fashion, come take a stand!"
With laughter that echoes, all creatures align,
As jellyfish shimmer, in costumes divine.

In dusk's gentle grip, all secrets are shared,
Salty sea breezes show how much they've cared,
In unspoken moments, life takes a pause,
As the ocean uncovers her playful cause.

Lonesome Voyage of the Moonlit Sea

A seagull sings with a cheesy grin,
Trying to catch a wave, but it's tough to win.
The moon winks down, with a cheeky chat,
While crabs dance up, waving their hat.

A fish swims by, wearing sunglasses cool,
While seaweed takes bets, playing the fool.
An octopus juggles, goofy and spry,
Splashing in laughter, beneath the night sky.

Waves giggle softly, tickling the sand,
While the starfish are plotting their next big band.
The dolphins dive deep, making funny faces,
In a splashy ballet of frolicsome paces.

And as the tide turns with giggles and sways,
The moon sails back, a bit lost in the rays.
Each ripple and wave holds a secret so spry,
Like a whispering joke, floating on high.

Reflective Traces of a Gentle Current

The current chuckles, listens, and sighs,
As fish trade jokes under bright, sunny skies.
A whale tells a tale, with laughter it sings,
While crabs tap dance on imaginary strings.

Shells hold court, their laughter a crest,
With turtles in bowties, looking their best.
A jellyfish giggles, floating like fluff,
Winking at currents, saying, "That's enough!"

The sand tickles toes, whispering glee,
As little fish school and shout, "Look at me!"
All under the surface, a frolicsome plight,
Where even the seaweed gets into the light.

And when night falls softly, like a quilted embrace,
The stars join the fun, shimmering in space.
This gentle current spins tales full of cheer,
Where laughter and ripples are always near.

Stillness Between the Skies and Tides

Between the waves, a joke is found,
A seagull's caw is the laugh's sweet sound.
Puddles reflect a silly old sun,
While barnacles giggle—oh, what fun!

Clouds parade slowly, puffed with delight,
As fish engage in a splashy light fight.
A dolphin swirls showing off with flair,
While the crabs applaud in their sandy chair.

Bubbles float up, pop with a cheer,
Tickling the toes of the waves down here.
The sun takes a bow, as the tide giggles wide,
Making ripples that dance, twirling with pride.

And as day ends, the ocean looks bright,
With laughter that twinkles in the soft twilight.
An encore of silence, a showstopper's tease,
In the hush of the water, we find our ease.

The Invisible Thread of Ocean Breezes

A breeze whirls around, playful and bold,
Whispering secrets that never grow old.
It tickles the sails, makes seagulls sway,
While fish flip and flop in a gleeful ballet.

The sun's golden rays, like confetti so bright,
Giggle with clouds, oh what a sight!
The seaweed sways, joining in with flair,
While the snappy shellfish are trying to share.

Ripples of laughter spread wide through the bay,
As salty seafoam begins its own play.
A crab pulls a prank, oh what a surprise!
As all of the currents do hearty high-fives.

In this breezy dance, the world feels so light,
As waves weave a tapestry, gleaming and bright.
With each tickle of breeze and each joyous wave,
It's a party of giggles, the ocean we crave.

The Peace That Lingers Where Waves Rest

On the beach where seagulls squawk,
A crab in a tuxedo takes a walk.
Shells gossip stories in a playful manner,
While starfish doze, like they have a planner.

Bubbles float like tiny balloons,
Jellyfish jiggle to the sound of tunes.
The sand tickles toes in a silly spree,
As a clam shouts, "Hey, don't step on me!"

Waves giggle as they crash and frolic,
Sneaky tides play hide and unlock.
Rubber ducks drift with a quirky grace,
While fish wear sunglasses, just to embrace.

And there's a dolphin with a wink so sly,
He flips and spins, oh my oh my!
In this place where laughter dances free,
Who knew the sea could be so funny?

Lapping Narratives of a Silent Shore

Tales are told by the shore's soft sigh,
Where conch shells whisper secrets high.
A clam with a pearl, and a wink in his eye,
Says, "I might be bumpy, but I'm never shy!"

The seaweed sways with exaggerated flair,
Pretending it's a celebrity at a fair.
As crabs do the shuffle, with sidesteps galore,
It's quite the party; just peek at the floor!

A starfish argues with the waves about height,
Saying, "I'm five-armed, and you're just alright!"
The seafoam giggles and splashes around,
As tide pools erupt with a bubbly sound.

Gulls swap stories, as they dive and dive,
In a feathered congress where all seem alive.
At this crafty coast, where jesters unite,
Every wave brings a grin, oh what a sight!

The Quiet Dance of Ocean Flora

Anemones sway like they're part of a show,
With colorful leotards, on the ocean's flow.
Kelp pirouettes while the barnacles cheer,
In this underwater ballet, there's nothing to fear.

Coral reefs gossip, with colors so bright,
They argue about who wears the best light.
An octopus chuckles, flipping through hues,
Saying, "I blend in with my fancy new shoes!"

Mollusks gossip with rhythm and grace,
As they shuffle together in this sea-spirited space.
Flotsam and jetsam applaud from afar,
Eagerly waiting for their own little star.

Sea cucumbers lounge, all casual and cool,
Monitoring the dance like a relaxed school.
In this watery waltz, with no need to care,
Even plankton's chuckling, just rolling on air!

Embracing the Abyss of Calm Waters

In the depths of tranquility, a sea cow floats,
Wearing sunglasses, and sipping sweet oats.
The anglerfish grins with a light in his eye,
Saying, "Come join me! Let's give it a try!"

Turtles play poker, with shells as their stakes,
While playful squids make a mess with their shakes.
Bubbles of laughter rise up to the top,
Echoing through currents, they spin and they bop.

In this quiet abyss, a clownfish jokes loud,
"Why so deep, my friends? Let's gather a crowd!"
Echoing chuckles ripple through the blue,
As the sea unfolds mysteries, both old and new.

Now a walrus tells tales, and they twist with flair,
All of them knowing, life's richer down there.
With gleeful abandon, they float and they twirl,
Even the sea urchins enjoy this swirl!

Hushed Hymn of the Surf

Waves whisper softly, a giggling tide,
They dance in circles, with foam as their guide.
Starfish chuckle, in their seaweed throne,
As mermaids gossip, in deep underwater tone.

Crabs wear hats made of kelp and sea leaves,
Giggling fish hide behind coral trees.
Seagulls squawk jokes, just to keep it light,
While snails race each other, with shells oh so bright.

The ocean hums tunes, both funny and sweet,
As jellyfish juggle, with grace in their feet.
The sand dollars laugh, with smiles on their face,
In waters so vast, it's a comical place.

Bubbles rise up, like balloons on parade,
As sea cucumbers roll, in the sea they wade.
They throw a grand party, beneath the blue sky,
With laughter and joy, as time passes by.

Dreaming Amidst the Tides

In pools of water, dreams take a nap,
As crabs tell tales, in their sandy trap.
A starfish yawns, stretching wide in the sun,
While dolphins play tag, just having some fun.

Turtles wear glasses, reading the tide,
As fish swim in circles, with nowhere to hide.
Seahorses dance, in a waltz that's quite slow,
While plankton do pirouettes, putting on a show.

The waves giggle softly, a tickle so bright,
With dolphins that leap, like they're taking a flight.
Shells trade stories, of sailors long gone,
As murky old eels slip out with a yawn.

The horizon grins, where sea meets the sky,
As the sun winks down, with a playful sigh.
In dreams of the deep, where silliness reigns,
A festival of laughter, where joy never wanes.

Repose Among the Coral

Coral castles stand, all painted with cheer,
Fish wear tuxedos, their parties sincere.
Anemones sway, with a rhythm so chill,
In the depths of the sea, with beauty they thrill.

Seashells gossip, like old friends at dawn,
Trading their stories, till the light is all gone.
An octopus juggles shells with a grin,
While clams clap their shells, cheering him in.

Bright colors abound, in a vibrant ballet,
As sponges just bounce, enjoying their stay.
A seahorse serves drinks, in a conch from the sea,
While moorish idols compete, "Come see me, come see!"

In a coral refrain, where silliness stirs,
The laughter of currents, like a song that occurs.
As waves softly cradle the joyful parade,
In repose, the sea's charm, forever displayed.

Silence Where the Sea Meets Sky

Where sea touches sky, the horizon takes pause,
A pelican swoops, but he's lost in applause.
With clouds making shapes of a giant green crab,
While fish tell tall tales, like a modern-day lab.

In ripples of blue, secrets flicker and float,
As barnacles tap dance on a driftwood boat.
The sun dips low, painting giggles in rays,
Whilst lazy old seals bask in sun's warm embrace.

A shorebird sings songs, with rhythm and flair,
As hermit crabs shuffle, showing their care.
Their shells hold the treasure of moments gone by,
In silence, they chuckle at clouds passing by.

All together they gather, for a whimsical show,
While the sea winks back, with a kindly hello.
Though silence surrounds, laughter bubbles beneath,
With a canvas so wide, it's a joy to bequeath.

Tranquil Waters

Bubbles rise with giggles, quite rare,
As fish debate who's the fairest there.
Seaweed dances to a tune we don't hear,
While crabs throw a party with plenty of cheer.

Seagulls shout their complaints up above,
While starfish plot a game of who they love.
The tide's in a hurry, it can't be too late,
As shells share secrets, debating their fate.

A dolphin jokes and flips with grace,
While octopuses try on a silly face.
The sandcastles crumble, but spirits are high,
With laughter that echoes, 'Oh my, oh my!'

In waters so calm, the jesters do wade,
As turtles play tag in a grand escapade.
With fins clapping joy, and shells as their stage,
It's a circus of creatures that's all the rage.

Timeless Tales

Waves whisper jokes from long ago,
While seashells chime in with giggles and glow.
The mermaids are plotting some mischief tonight,
With fish on the side, they take to flight.

Clams hold court, with a pearl for a crown,
Debating who wears the silliest frown.
"Turn left at the reef, we might find treasure!"
"Or just more barnacles, what a true pleasure!"

Whales sing softly, but change to a dance,
Their rhythm will make the sea creatures prance.
An eel slips and ducks to avoid the glare,
Of a crab throwing shade, trying to snare.

Ahoy there, it's a tale that never grows old,
Of friendship and laughter under the fold.
With twinkling stars laughing down from above,
This world is a canvas, painted with love.

Reflections in a Quiet Pool

Ripples create art in the sunlit bay,
As minnows perform in a comical play.
The lily pads giggle as frogs jump around,
While turtles roll laughter, their joy knows no bound.

Serenity whispers, but don't be deceived,
Fish wear tiny hats, you'd never believe!
A dragonfly dances, shaky, yet bold,
With stories of mishaps in colors of gold.

The sun offers warmth, like a toast to the day,
While snails recite poetry in their own way.
The reeds sway to rhythms, they can't keep still,
As nature hums softly with each little thrill.

In the quiet, all antics unfold in delight,
If you listen closely, it's pure, sheer insight.
For laughter in stillness can truly be found,
In reflections of joy that forever abound.

Stillness in the Embrace of the Blue

The still blue whispers with a cheeky grin,
As fish wear sunglasses, soaking in fin.
Coral reefs chuckle, so vibrant and bright,
Under the waves where all things feel right.

Crabs with top hats, strutting with pride,
In ballrooms of sand where the sea critters glide.
Jellyfish float in a gooey ballet,
While clams keep the beat, come join the soiree!

The seals pull some pranks, while dolphins do flips,
With mermaids in tutus, it's a party that rips.
With tides that just giggle, and bubbles that pop,
This sea of pure silliness just won't ever stop.

The stillness is filled with jokes shared in fun,
Making memories under the gleaming sun.
And oh, take a seat, for you won't want to leave,
This laughter surrounds us, we just have to believe.

Cradle of the Forgotten Deep

Down in the depths where the silliness sleeps,
Creatures hold meetings and share their big leaps.
A narwhal with glasses explains the old lore,
While clownfish giggle and call for encore!

Eels swap old tales of shimmies and snores,
They twist and they twirl, asking for roars.
A mirror of bubbles reflects all the fun,
Where seaweed and barnacles dance 'til they're done.

A hermit crab's throwing a shell-borrowing spree,
"Who'll trade their abode? Come on, come see!"
They chatter away, making waves filled with cheer,
As jellyfish flaunt every color, oh dear!

In the hush of the deep, such antics abound,
In laughter and play, true joy can be found.
The cradle of silliness, where legends all seep,
Is hidden quite well in the ocean's deep sweep.

Subdued Symphonies of the Waters

The waves begin to softly hum,
The fish swim by, they look so dumb.
They dance and glide without a care,
While seagulls squawk an off-key air.

The starfish lounge, so very chill,
Their daily job is just to grill.
They sunbathe on a rocky seat,
And laugh at crabs with dancing feet.

Jellyfish float, so bright and bold,
With jiggly moves, their story's told.
They wave goodbye with tentacles wide,
And play hide and seek, oh what a ride!

The ocean's prank, a charming tease,
With whispers wrapped among the breeze.
A wacky song, a watery joke,
Where every ripple starts to poke.

Glistening Calm of the Abyss

Deep down where light is just a dream,
The fish are planning quite a scheme.
They'll throw a party, what a sight,
And invite the squid, it's a wild night!

With swirls of glitter, they take a chance,
The sea cucumbers join in the dance.
They wiggle and giggle, spread delight,
While crabs in tuxedos roam the night.

An octopus serves drinks, so sly,
With many arms, they're oh so spry.
The bubbles pop like laughter's tone,
While sea anemones bemoan alone.

In long-lost corners, secrets flow,
With hints of jokes, they ebb and glow.
An underwater tale, quite absurd,
As laughter spreads without a word.

The Quiet Embrace of Celestial Tides

The moonlight winks upon the sea,
The whales are giggling, can't you see?
They sing in jumbles, notes unkind,
And watch the seashells lose their mind.

A dolphin juggles with great flair,
While fish all cheer, "It's quite the air!"
With splashes loud and graceful bows,
They're cutting up, as only pros.

Crabs click-clack like they're in a band,
While seaweed sways, it's oh so grand.
But snails complain of moving slow,
While turtles roll their eyes and go.

So in this realm, where whimsy reigns,
The sea reflects our silly chains.
A canvas blue of joyful quirks,
Where laughter swims and fun just lurks.

Serenity of the Crystal Depths

Under water where the giggles splash,
The sea stars wink in a frantic dash.
The otters float with silly grins,
While sea horses play out their spins.

From coral reefs, the jokes emerge,
A banquet feast, oh what a surge!
Pirates pass with chests of gold,
But all they've found is seaweed rolled.

A bubble rises with tales to tell,
Of crabs who steal and think it's swell.
While starry nights with glee collide,
As undercurrents support the ride.

This aqua realm, with joys abound,
Laughing echoes all around.
So when you seek a funny tune,
Just listen close, the depths croon!

Echoes of Tranquility

Waves whisper secrets, oh so sly,
Fish in tuxedos swim by,
Seagulls giggle with a flair,
As crusty crabs dance without a care.

Sandcastles tumble with each swell,
A clam laughs at the ocean's yell,
Beach balls bounce with glee,
The tide rolls in, we're all carefree.

Seashells chat with a gossip's delight,
While starfish show off under the light,
The water's deep, but so is the jest,
Every splash is just a playful quest.

The lighthouse grins at the silly shores,
As dolphins juggle and the sea-snakes snore,
In this watery realm, life is a game,
Where laughter echoes, and joy is the name.

Murmurs of the Blue Abyss

Bubbles pop like jokes in the sea,
Crabs wear hats, oh look at me!
An octopus waves, six arms to flaunt,
While sea turtles gossip, they surely do taunt.

The anemones dance, such gentle sways,
As fish tell tales of their wacky days,
A snorkeler snorts, laughter fills the air,
While jellyfish jive without any care.

Seashells play music with a sea breeze,
Each note tickles our toes with ease,
Underwater, the jokes are quite grand,
In this world, the silliness expands.

As waves roll in with a cheeky grin,
Life below sparkles, where joy begins,
With every splash, our hearts just beam,
In the abyss, we all share a dream.

Rhythm of the Endless Tide

A crab taps dance while the tide takes a bow,
Shells keep the beat; take a look at that cow!
Fish swim in circles, making a line,
While mermaids giggle, sipping on brine.

The waves chuckle softly, a watery cheer,
As swimming trunks tumble, oh my, oh dear!
In sync with the surf, a rhythm so bold,
Where ticklish sand is a sight to behold.

With every new wave, the silliness grows,
Seagulls drop selfies, striking a pose,
Laughter erupts with each frothy crash,
The ocean's a stage, where humor's a splash.

When the sun dips low with a wink and a nod,
Dancing waves tell jokes, oh my, how they prod!
In this perfect blend, we twirl and glide,
To the rhythm of laughter, the endless tide.

Lullaby of Silent Horizons

Stars peek out where the sea meets the sky,
Fish whisper dreams as they float on by,
A sleepy surf sings a chuckling tune,
While crabs in pajamas dance under the moon.

The waves play tag with the sandy shore,
As barnacles giggle, "Can you take more?"
A buoy bobs, wearing a stubborn frown,
As sea swallows tease, "You'll never drown!"

Shells hum lullabies with a gentle sway,
While rays of sun cast shadows at play,
In the twilight glow, all worries cease,
The horizon chuckles, wrapping us in peace.

In the stillness, where laughter finds rest,
With sea breezes playing, life's at its best,
So let the world hush, hear the light-hearted call,
In this lullaby realm, we can all have a ball.

www.ingramcontent.com/pod-product-compliance
Lightning Source LLC
Chambersburg PA
CBHW060128230426
43661CB00003B/365